"As a rental property owner and entrepreneur for over 14 years one of the biggest risks most of us have is not being properly insured to protect not only our investment but also our entire financial future. It's easy for us to think of new ways to make money but we often put little thought to our insurance. Ryan's book should be required reading for any real estate investors, (yes, including all you wholesalers out there) on exactly what insurance you need, why, how much, and when. This book could save you thousands from overpaying for the wrong insurance and potentially even more by having the right insurance when you need it the most. If you're not 1000% confident in your insurance situation, read this book now, give Ryan a call, and get protected."

-**Trevor Mauch**, CEO of *Carrot.com* | *Inc 500/5000 #699*

"If you are a real estate investor you need to read Ryan Ingram's book. As investors we find that we have to go through a lot of trial and error. Ryan Ingram is the real deal and the information he's provided is much needed as it relates to your real estate investing and insurance"

-**Renard Owens**, CEO *Axe Capital Investments LLC*

"Wow, Ryan has created a real value add resource for any real estate investor, no matter how long you've been in the business. I've been investing in real estate for

almost 20 years and learned a lot from this book. I'll be doing a policy review tomorrow, thanks Ryan!!"
-**Mike Vann**, CEO *Mission Capital Group*

"If you are looking for a quick read that's extremely comprehensive and will enlighten you as it relates to investment property insurance, my friend Ryan Ingram does an amazing job with this book. "
-**Aaron T Walker**, president and founder of *View From The Top*

"If you're a real estate investor, you want to read this book! It is rare to find great resources that speak directly to the needs of a specific community, but Ryan has taken the broad topic of "insurance" and speaks DIRECTLY to real estate investors. He speaks from first-hand experience in real estate and a solid background in insurance. He brings truth to light for the real estate investors that want to protect and enhance their real estate portfolio by using insurance the right way. Once you read this book, you will be better equipped to grow, protect, and enhance your life through your real estate holdings."
-**Rich Allen**, Business Advisor and Real Estate Investor

"Knowledge is power! As a new investor, I have found Ryan's book extremely helpful in making sound decisions regarding the insurance of my properties. There is so much to learn in this business and my good friend Ryan takes the subject of insurance and makes it fun and easy to understand from an investor's standpoint. This is a

must-read for any Real Estate Investor – new or seasoned veteran!"
-**Steve Spence**, *S² Invest LLC*

"Easy read, informative and clears up some of the insurance questions I have been pondering for years."
-**Steven VanCauwenbergh**, www.savvyradioshow.com

"It's hard to overstate the importance of insuring your rental property at the right level. Every investor needs to weigh their own tolerance for risk against the expense of coverage. To do this, you must be able to decipher industry jargon and understand the basics. This is where Ryan Ingram's book "Rental Property Insurance" comes in. It's a great primer on property insurance, and it provides the explanations necessary to make informed decisions."
–**Brian Murray**, author of *Crushing It in Apartments and Commercial Real Estate*

"This book does a great job of breaking down a seemingly complicated industry to the core basics we need to understand as investors. I wish I could have read this when I started real estate investing two decades ago, it would have saved me a ton of headaches and $$."
-**Darrin Carey**, *Dayton Capital Partners, LLC*

"As a real estate investor and insurance expert, Ryan's book covers it all! Now there is a source and reference guide that explains the types of coverage you need, why you need it, along with excellent examples that are easy to understand. This book is required reading for any serious real estate investor."

-**Mike Hanna**, *Investmark Mortgage, LLC*

"As an investor myself, I assure you that you will not find a more comprehensive handbook on insuring investment property than this book! If you are an investor, or considering becoming one, take some time to digest this important information to avoid years of costly mistakes."

-**Debra White**, broker at *Roost Real Estate Co.*

"I specialize in the real estate investment industry as a buy-and-hold investor and as a tax specialist CPA – where majority of my clients invest in many different types of real estate. I have had the privilege of getting to know Ryan over the last year and he is a special individual. He is a genuine person with extreme passion for his job in the insurance world and as a real estate investor. The book Ryan put together is just as passionate and genuine as he is. You will learn a lot about insurance and about Ryan in a quick and easy read. I'm excited for everyone to get to know more about Ryan and insurance."

-**Phil Weickert**, CPA at *Strategic Tax Services & Modern Edge Lease LLC*

"As a seasoned real estate investor the importance of property insurance can not be over emphasized. Ryan's insurance knowledge combined with his real estate acumen is invaluable to investors balancing expenses with financial performance. I seek Ryan's business advice on all insurance topics and he constantly provides value in this critical component of property ownership."

 -**Lane Beene,** Managing Partner at *Pilot Legacy Private Equity Group*

RENTAL
PROPERTY
INSURANCE

AN INVESTOR'S GUIDE TO INSURANCE

RYAN INGRAM

Legal Disclaimer and Terms of Use

This book is presented solely for educational and informational purposes. The author and publisher are not offering it as legal, insurance, or other professional services advice. While best efforts have been used in preparing this book, the author and publisher make no representations or warranties of any kind and assume no liabilities of any kind with respect to the accuracy or completeness of the contents and specifically disclaim any implied warranties of merchantability or fitness of use for a particular purpose.

Neither the author nor the publisher shall be held liable or responsible to any person or entity with respect to any loss or incidental or consequential damages caused, or alleged to have been caused, directly or indirectly, by the information or programs contained herein. No warranty may be created or extended by sales representatives or written sales materials. This information is not intended as professional advice, as professional advice must be tailored to the specific circumstances and facts of each situation. Consult an insurance professional before taking any action based on information contained herein. Keep in mind that insurance laws and practices vary from state to state.

Any stories, characters, or entities, contained in this work are fictional. Any likeness to an actual person, either living or dead, is strictly coincidental.

ISBN: 9781733152105

To my wife, whose undying and unconditional love, support and expert matriarchal skills allows me the freedom to chase our dreams, better our lives and our communities.

...Also, Mom. You're pretty cool too. And Dad, thanks for making me an Ingram.

CONTENTS

INTRODUCTION

Purchasing insurance for your rental properties can be complicated. Especially if you're new to the real estate investing world. With all the variables that can go into every insurance policy, it can be easy to just call the agent that took care of your insurance policy on your personal residence, and do whatever she recommends. You might even just do a quick google search and pick the insurance company with the lowest rates.

Unfortunately, as I've seen over and over again, when investors get around to purchasing insurance they usually fall victim to one of two categories:

1.   They over-insure their properties and pay much more than they need to each month; or

2.   They under-insure their properties and then it comes back to bite them when they need to file a claim.

No investor wants to find themselves in either of these scenarios, but there aren't many resources that help investors understand insurance so they can make educated choices about their policies.

That's where this book comes in. By the time you finish it, not only will you understand the basics of investment property insurance, but you'll be armed with the tools you need when fishing for your policy.

Now, before we get into insurance basics, let me tell you a little bit about myself.

I am obsessed with real estate investing - specifically, what it provides for both my family and our lifestyle. But that wasn't always the case. I used to be obsessed with the stock market. Since I was 17 I read every book on finance I could get my hands on. I had even formulated a retirement plan for myself: accumulate enough diversified dividend stocks to be financially free.

That all changed in 2015.

At that time I was in law enforcement. One day I responded to an attempted break-in. Once everything settled, I struck up a casual conversation with the homeowner. It turns out he was the owner of a very successful local business. My interest piqued, I began asking questions about his business. But, I quickly discovered he wasn't interested in speaking about his business. Instead, he wanted to talk about the neighborhood.

We spoke about the local streets, different houses for sale, various problem neighborhoods, and streets in the area that I would be alright with my family residing. At first, I didn't understand the significance, but he quickly revealed that he loved real estate investing and was looking for more places to purchase properties.

Within a few weeks, he took me around to his commercial and residential properties. At each place, he was kind enough to walk me through how much he paid, how much it rented for, the problems he was having, and how he was working through them.

Intellectually, this rocked my world. I was stumped. I was all-in on stock market investing. But I couldn't stop running through the conversations I'd had with that business owner - over and over again.

Over the next few days, I crunched all of the numbers I could come up with, comparing real estate investing and investing in the stock market.

Real estate won every single time, but I didn't want to admit that I was wrong. I was so vested in educating myself about the stock market, financial trends, etc., that putting the stock market behind me and focusing on real estate felt like turning my back on a lover.

Almost begrudgingly, I started reading books on real estate investing. I listened to podcasts and consumed any material I could find on the topic. I had one mission - to prove to myself that investing in the stock market was superior to real estate.

That never happened.

What I found was the more I learned about real estate, the less appealing the stock market became.

I decided to throw out my previous retirement plan and start over. But I didn't want to just start over. I decided to change careers. I stepped away from law enforcement and started, of all things, an insurance agency.

If you're curious why I jumped into insurance, here's why. Insurance is a relationship-based industry dependent upon professionals with ethics, a high moral compass, and integrity.

While selling insurance, I continued my real estate investing education. I listened to all of the BiggerPockets podcasts and read all of the books they recommended. Then, in August of 2017, I took the plunge and bought my first duplex. I couldn't resist including the picture I had my cousin take after we closed.

In 2018, I purchased 24 more doors (primarily single-family homes) and in 2019 (so far), I've purchased 14 doors.

When I began digging into real estate investing, I immediately noticed that the investing and insurance two worlds didn't work well together. I had a difficult time writing policies on my properties that accurately reflected my investment strategy. So, I started asking questions to other insurance agents and underwriters at insurance companies.

I quickly found that almost no one was familiar with the complexities that came with insuring investment homes. Many brokers avoided real estate investors altogether.

That had to change, and since no one seemed like they wanted to plow the way, I figured it would have to be me. I'm not claiming to have all the answers. In fact, the more I learn, the more I realize how much I do not know. But, I wrote this book to start the conversation between investors and insurance agents. I knew I had to do my part to empower the investor to learn how to utilize insurance intelligently - to increase his or her return on investment and protect his legacy and financial freedom against liability claims and natural disasters.

Now, let's get on with the good stuff.

INVESTOR'S INSURANCE POLICY QUICK-REFERENCE GUIDE:

Before getting into any sort of details or terms, let's discuss what type of policies that come up for different types of investment strategies.

House Hackers (1-4 units): Homeowner's Policy[1]

Buy and Hold: Dwelling Fire[2]

Fix and Flip: Vacant Policy[3]

Wholesaler/Wholetail: General Liability[4]

---

[1] If you plan to purchase - or have already purchased - a multifamily (1-4 units) property and plan to live in one of the units, you need a homeowners policy.

[2] The term "dwelling fire" refers to the insurance policy for any residential property that is not owner-occupied. Now that you know it, you should use this term regularly. It is both catchy and fun to say.

[3] If you are purchasing a property to renovate and then resell, you will need what the insurance world calls a "vacant" policy. These are generally 2-3 times the price of normal policies and are available for monthly, 3-month, 6-month, and annual terms.

[4] No additional insurance policy is needed if you will never take ownership of the property. If you take ownership of the property and it's unoccupied, a vacant policy; if occupied, a dwelling fire policy

Apartment Complex: Either a business owners policy (abbreviated as "BOP" in the insurance world) or a commercial package policy (CPP)[5]

Vacation Rentals and Airbnb: Dwelling Fire[6]

Student Housing, Sober-living, Assisted Living: General Liability and Dwelling Fire if residential or BOP/CPP if commercial.[7]

Turnkey Providers: General Liability and each property must be insured. [8]

New Construction: General Liability & Builders' Risk [9]

With this and the downloadable infographic on the next page, you're well on your way to becoming a savvy real estate investor.

---

[5] Any property either 5 units or greater will most likely be required to be written on a commercial policy. Any property with retail space, regardless of the number of units, will be written on a commercial policy.

[6] General Liability and when needed, force placed (lender placed) insurance.

[7] Properties used for these purposes will most likely need to be insured on the non-admitted market.

[8] You can insure each property individually with a vacant policy or if you have several open projects, a blanket builders risk policy may be the better option.

[9] If you will be building properties and selling them, you'll want a general liability policy. This is true even if you are using a general contractor for the construction. You'll also want a builders risk policy to protect the property and materials as it is being built. If you are building properties and keeping them as a buy and hold, you'll only need the builders risk policy.

Now, here are some things to think about now that we've covered the basics:

1.   What kind of investor are you?

2.   What type of real estate investments are you interested in?

3.   Familiarize yourself with the policy and terms that are recommended for your strategy, even write it down so that you have a good starting place on what to ask for when you are speaking with a licensed insurance professional.

WHAT TYPE OF POLICY DO I NEED?

INGRAM INSURANCE

HOUSE HACKERS (1-4 UNITS)
HOMEOWNER'S POLICY

APARTMENT COMPLEX
BUSINESSOWNERS (BOP)/
COMMERCIAL (CPP) POLICY

BUY AND HOLD
DWELLING FIRE

VACATION RENTALS/AIRBNB
DWELLING FIRE

FIX AND FLIP
VACANT POLICY

TURNKEY PROVIDERS
GENERAL LIABILITY

WHOLESALER/WHOLETAIL
GENERAL LIABILITY

NEW CONSTRUCTION
GENERAL LIABILITY/BUILDERS' RISK

For future reference, you can download this worksheet at www.insuredbyingram.com/download

SIMILARITIES WITH HOMEOWNERS AND DWELLING FIRE POLICIES

I speak with a decent amount of investors that are not quite sure of the differences between the homeowners policies and the dwelling fire policies. I've even had a few that thought homeowners policies received favorable pricing, so they wanted to lie about who lived there!

If you're reading this, I know you're above this and wouldn't lie about such an infinitesimal matter. Personally, I don't think any price variance is worth my integrity. Nonetheless, confusion and bad information cause people to do strange things.

All joking aside, homeowners policies and dwelling fire policies are very similar. But, they have their distinct differences. Before we discuss those differences, we need to set up the framework around how they are written and their common denominators.

The three different concepts we need to first discuss are the differences between **basic**, **broad**, and **special form**; the differences between the settlement options of Actual Cash Value and Replacement Cost; and finally the various coverage letters that represent different coverages included in your insurance policy.

Let's dive into these over the next few chapters and remember, if it is confusing or you want more information, don't hesitate to reach out to me. I can almost guarantee the conversation will make my day; ryan@insuredbyingram.com

BASIC, BROAD, AND SPECIAL FORM OPTIONS

Homeowners and dwelling fire policy forms come in three different options: basic, broad, and special form. Every real estate investor NEEDS TO KNOW the difference between these three forms. Put another way, the form determines how, if at all, a claim is paid out.

To have a decent conversation about this, there is a term you need to be familiar with: peril.

Peril simply means the cause of loss. Here are some examples:

- Fire
- Wind
- Hail
- Ice Weight

Just remember that anything that can cause damage or loss to your property is a peril.

Both basic and broad forms are referred to as "Named Peril" forms. What this means is that in order for a claim to be paid out, the peril MUST FIRST BE SPECIFICALLY LISTED on the policy form. In other words, and this is the most important part, if a specific peril is not listed on the policy form, the claim WILL NOT BE PAID out.

I'll give you an outrageous example, just for fun: if a wild pig flew through your property, and the property was covered with a Named Peril form, the policy would need to explicitly state that it covers physical damage caused by wild flying pigs. Without the flying pigs being named in the policy, you would be out of luck if you tried to file a claim.

Special form is what is called an "Open Peril" form. This form operates in exactly the opposite manner of a named peril form. With special form, everything that could happen to your property is covered unless it is SPECIFICALLY EXCLUDED on the form. Using the wild flying pig example once more, you can be assured that this is covered unless your policy specifically states that it will not cover any damage caused by wild flying pigs.

To further illustrate these forms, here is a comparison table that generalizes policy forms. Like all other information in this book, this is not specific to your policy or meant to be all-inclusive. You need to consult your insurance agent and your policy to confirm what coverages you do and do not have. If you'd like to keep it around and reference it at will, you can download a copy at www.insuredbyingram.com/download

CAUSES OF LOSS FORMS – COMPARISON CHART

CAUSES OF LOSS	BASIC (10 10)	BROAD (10 20)	SPECIAL (10 30)
Fire	X	X	X
Lightning	X	X	X
Explosion	X	X	X
Windstorm or Hail *	X	X	X
Smoke	X	X	X
Aircraft or Vehicles **	X	X	X
Riot or Civil Commotion	X	X	X
Vandalism *	X	X	X
Sprinkler Leakage *	X	X	X
Sinkhole Collapse	X	X	X
Volcanic Action	X	X	X
Additional Coverage – Limited Coverage for "Fungus", Wet Rot, Dry Rot and Bacteria	X	X	X
Falling Objects		X	X
Weight of Snow, Ice or Sleet		X	X
Water Damage		X	X
Additional Coverage – Collapse		X	X
Theft			X
Direct Physical Loss			X

* Windstorm or Hail, Vandalism, and Sprinkler Leakage may be individually excluded by endorsement

** Exclusion for vehicles owned/operated by named insured

SETTLEMENT OPTIONS: ACTUAL CASH VALUE VS. REPLACEMENT COST

The concept of having insurance revolves around mitigating the risk of loss. If you have a loss, you expect to receive money from the insurance company to return you to the same position you were in prior to that loss - no more, no less. The insurance companies calculate the money that you will receive in a few different ways. The two most common are "Actual Cash Value" and "Replacement Cost." Both of these options are a bit more convoluted than they appear, and neither of them has anything to do with how much you paid for the property. But that's why you're here. So, let's get started.

Replacement Cost

If you call ten different insurance companies, you'll most likely get ten different Replacement Cost Estimates (RCE) for your property. Most insurance companies have Replacement Cost calculators embedded into their websites or quoting systems. These systems gather public information to form an estimate on how much it would cost to rebuild the property - in the event of a total loss - with like materials. The information gathered includes basic residential information such as square feet, number of kitchens, and bathrooms. It also assumes the building materials used given the year of construction. These calculators then factor in the cost of all materials and labor required to rebuild the home exactly as it was originally. This includes outdated materials, inflation, and techniques that may no longer be up to code.

These estimates are also pretty flexible as you can adjust the types of building materials and quality of finish. It generally isn't difficult to increase or decrease these estimates by a few thousand and it generally doesn't affect the premium too greatly.

Here is an example of when this might come into play.

One of the most common drastic changes in older properties is changing the wall type from plaster to drywall. This generally reduces the amount of the Replacement Cost and can have an impact on the amount the policy costs the investor.

To summarize: if you are insuring your property on a Replacement Cost basis, the cost calculation will spit out a number that theoretically represents all the materials and labor needed to get the property back to its original condition.

The replacement cost has nothing to do with the amount that you paid for the property or the amount that you feel the property is worth. For example, I have a duplex that I purchased for $35,000 in 2017. This property is insured at a Replacement Cost of $307,000. If a total loss were to occur - say the building burned to the ground - I would then have a budget of $307,000, which would include demolition, clean-up, materials, and labor necessary to rebuild the property to its condition prior to the fire.

As you're reading this, it's possible that the thought of burning the property down to collect the insurance money crossed your mind. That is exactly why insurance companies are apprehensive about insuring rental properties at replacement cost that were recently acquired for a substantially lower amount than the Replacement Cost calculation.

Insurance companies call this a "moral hazard," and want to do their part in limiting your temptation to commit arson. Depending on the comfort level an insurance company, the condition of the property, or merely the purchase price, you may not be able to get a replacement cost policy until after you have had the property for a few years, or you've made repairs.

Actual Cash Value

The Actual Cash Value formula is an entirely different animal than the replacement cost value. Actual cash value is very commonly abbreviated as ACV, so we are going to do that in this book. Here is the formula: replacement cost - depreciation = actual cash value. A general rule of thumb (not always accurate) to calculate depreciation is 1% per year to a maximum of 50%.

Let's use the example of my duplex again, I purchased it for $35,000 in 2017; it was built in 1900 and the Replacement Cost is $307,000. Since this property was built 119 years ago, it will surpass the max depreciation of 50%. So we will divide 307,000 by 2 to get $153,500.

In the event of a total loss, like the building burning down, I would receive a check for $153,500. Most likely, this would not replace the structure as it stands, and it would not be sufficient to rebuild. However, I could use this to clean up the mess, sell the land, and purchase another similar property.

As we are speaking in terms of a total loss, the difference between ACV and RC is just a matter of how much money you'll be walking away with. In my opinion, the largest exposure and difference between the different settlement options comes in the event of a partial loss. Let us continue building on the previous example, but change it to a partial loss instead of a total loss.

A kitchen-fire destroys the kitchen in one of the two units. In order to complete all of the repairs, it would cost $45,000. This is within both the RC limit of $307,000 and ACV limit of $153,500. Under the Replacement Cost policy, you would receive the entire amount of $45,000 and you would probably end up with a much nicer kitchen than you started off with.

However, with the ACV policy, depreciation will be factored into the loss. If we were to apply the rule of thumb, the total amount would be adjusted with a 50%

decrease. Under the ACV policy, you would receive around $27,500 to make the repairs.

Some investors that have either dedicated contractors or who do the work themselves are comfortable with this. There isn't a right or wrong way to pick your policy. It all depends on how much risk you are willing to shoulder and take responsibility for.

As an insurance agent, it is always easier to recommend clients to go with the Replacement Cost policy. You'll get better coverage and in the event of a loss, you will most likely receive more money than it takes to repair the property. If you have an ACV policy and you're not fully aware of the implications, you may potentially be very upset at the time of a loss.

Just remember that, depending on the price and condition of the property, an ACV policy may be your only option until you've either seasoned the property or made the appropriate repairs.

If you want more information on the differences between Replacement Cost and Actual Cash Value, feel free to email me at: ryan@insuredbyingram.com otherwise, let's talk about the next topic, coverage letters.

COVERAGE LETTERS

Homeowners and dwelling fire policies share coverage letters on policy forms. This means that both of these policies commonly have coverages A through F. You need to know what these coverage letters are to ensure you're properly protected. But don't worry, they aren't complicated.

They're just letters.

If you were to look at your homeowner's policy, you'll see something like, "Coverage A: Dwelling Value." Some companies have stopped putting "Coverage A" on policy forms completely; instead, you'll just see "Dwelling Value," followed by the amount your property is insured for.

Don't overthink it. There is power and freedom in understanding how your investments are covered in the event of a loss. Let's briefly discuss these so you can familiarize yourself with the policies.

Coverage A, dwelling limit, is the dollar amount which the primary building is covered. Lenders generally require this amount to be greater than what you paid for the property. If you purchase a property for $100,000, the lender will want Coverage A to be greater than the loan amount. This is the amount which covers all of the building materials. If the policy is going to be settled at replacement cost, you should expect this number to be the amount it would cost to replace all building materials and the labor necessary to rebuild the property.

Coverage B, other structures, includes any additional property on the parcel. This can be a garage, shed, and even fences. If you have a giant garage with an apartment above it, you'd most likely want to increase the amount of this coverage. This coverage is not automatically included on some dwelling fire policies, so you will want to double-check before signing the policy to make sure your additional structures are covered.

Coverage C, personal property, is included for your personal belongings. In homeowners policies, this covers couches, jewelry, guns, whatever else you might have. For rentals, this covers the investor's property and can be applied to appliances or other investor-provided contents.[10]

Coverage D, loss of use or loss of rents, is a very helpful coverage. In the event that a covered loss occurs (refer to basic, broad, and special forms) Coverage D will step in and either pay for additional living expenses or loss of rents for the minimum amount of time while the property is renovated or repaired.

Coverage E, personal liability, is the general liability section and is broken up into both Per

---

[10] This does not cover the tenant's personal property. If they want their personal property covered, they will have to purchase a renters insurance policy (HO-4).

Occurrence and per year or Aggregate totals. General liability coverages protect against liability claims for personal injury, bodily injury, or other mishaps that may happen on or around the property. If someone got hurt on your property, and wanted to sue you it would come out of this portion of the policy.

Coverage F, medical payments, is very similar to the medical payments coverage on auto policies. This covers the immediate medical expenses for those hurt while on the property premises. This is primarily used to try to nip potential lawsuits in the bud so they do not blossom into giant liability claims under Coverage E. Some insurance agents, jokingly call this "I'm sorry, don't sue me" money.

That wraps it up for the commonly used coverage letters. Now we can start talking about the different investment strategies and the corresponding policies they should be written on. As always, for more information, reach out to me at ryan@insuredbyingram.com.

HOUSE HACKERS AND THE HOMEOWNERS POLICY

Homeowners policies are generally more robust than dwelling fire policies. Insurance companies like to throw in additional coverages to make the policy well-rounded and provide fuller coverage to the homeowner. However, to the real estate investor, a lot of these extra coverages are unnecessary and make little difference in the long run.

Additionally, insurance companies are generally more lax on the underwriting because of the implied "pride of ownership" factor, that most home buyers experience. With some companies, the homeowners policy may even have a preferential rating and be cheaper than a dwelling fire policy.

In order to be eligible for a homeowners policy, the property must be between 1 and 4 units and it cannot have any commercial exposure, such as a retail space or a storefront. Real estate investors with an LLC also need to watch out here. If you purchased the property, even though you're living in it, and you did it inside of your LLC, there is a chance you may not be eligible to get a homeowners policy.

The main advantage of insuring an investment property that you are house-hacking is that the homeowners policy will include content coverage. Most people, not necessarily the wise and thrifty house hacker, have a lot of personal belongings they carry around with them from home to home. The homeowners policy will include coverage either Replacement Cost or Actual Cash Value for the insured personal items.

If the property is ineligible for a homeowners policy and is insured on a dwelling fire policy, be aware this policy does not provide any coverage for your personal belongings. If the property is purchased in an LLC and you live there, and if you'd like coverage for your content, it may benefit you to also get a renters policy at the same location.

Each homeowners policy comes in basic, broad, and special forms. These are usually abbreviated HO1, HO2, and HO3; it is very rare to come across an HO1 policy. It is most common for a homeowners policy to be written on special form as an HO3. Please refer to the previous comparison chart to determine what form would be best for you.

Chances are, there is little price difference between the HO2 and HO3. There is also an HO5 (comprehensive, which is greater than special), however, this is most likely unnecessary for a property that you are house hacking.

BUY AND HOLD: DWELLING FIRE

My favorite quote from Gary Keller's "Millionaire Real Estate Investor" is, "all roads lead to buy and hold." In my personal experience and hearing from other investors, this couldn't be truer. Flipping homes, wholesaling, etc., are generally means to raise capital to acquire rentals to hold long term. Consequently, the dwelling fire policy may be the most important policy to have an understanding of.

As previously discussed, the dwelling fire policy is available on three different forms: basic, broad, and special form. I'd highly recommend that you go back and review the comparison chart and find your comfort level (Also, download a copy for your perpetual reference at www.insuredbyingram.com/download).

In addition, there are at least two settlement options, either Actual Cash Value, or Replacement Cost. Every investor is unique and has his or her own set of standards and expectations. I have clients that do not want insurance to get involved in any way unless the house completely burns down. These clients like to carry $10,000 deductibles and they only want to hedge against catastrophic losses; anything less and they will take personal responsibility for and treat it as a line-item on their budget. If they do have a catastrophic loss, they do not want to rebuild the property. Instead, they would but rather acquire another similar property elsewhere.

I also have clients that want anything that could possibly happen to a property to be covered at full Replacement Cost. They are generally attached to an area and, regardless of the purchase price of the property, want to rebuild the property to its original condition, or better. Commonly, these are clients that purchase a new home and retain their previous home as a rental.

Regardless of what your comfort level is, I encourage everyone to choose a higher deductible. For real estate investments, I generally like to start at a deductible of $2,500 and work my way up depending on the client's comfort level. This is my choice for two reasons - price and efficiency.

In quoting with different companies, $2,500 is generally the sweet spot for getting the best rate. Increasing the deductible beyond this doesn't cause a substantial amount of annual savings on one property. However, if you have several properties on one policy, it may be worthwhile to look at higher deductibles.

On the claims side, in terms of efficiency, filing small claims tends to be counterproductive. The larger your portfolio, and the more assets you have to insure, the more selective you want to be in filing claims. This is true for both your personal policies and the policies on your investments. All insurance companies share giant databases full of everyone's information and history. If you have small claims on your reports, there is a surcharge that will impact all of your policies and raise the rates for anything you own. Even having a large claim, completely out of your control, will make you difficult to insure for 3 to 5 years.

As a general rule of thumb, you should do all that you can avoid filing a claim. If you can utilize some of your CapEx resources or repairs and maintenance fund rather than filing, do it. Take as much responsibility for your properties as possible and use insurance as an absolute last resort.

A common question or request that I get is to put all properties an individual owns on one policy to save a couple of dollars. Generally, I have not found this to be true - most companies willing to put several properties on one policy will charge the same per location whether it is a stand-alone policy or grouped with others. Companies that specialize in investment properties are going to be incredibly competitive on price already, compared to other companies that only allow for one property per policy.

To me, the main appeal of having all properties on one policy is convenience - one policy, one bill, one giant stack of documents to keep up with. However, there are a few hindrances in placing all properties on one policy. The two main difficulties are the deeded owner and mortgages and escrow billing.

In order to be on one policy, most companies want all of the properties to be deeded to the same entity. Even if all of the entities are sole member LLCs, or all LLCs have the same ownership structure, they will be required to have separate policies. I have several clients that form a new LLC for each property they own; while this may be a beneficial strategy from an attorney or liability perspective, it doesn't transfer smoothly to the insurance realm.

The second issue that arises is from the mortgage and billing side of the policy. There is only one billing account for each policy. So, if there are multiple properties on one policy, this can create an issue for the lender. If you are paying for the insurance out of your escrow account with the lender, the amount in escrow will only cover the property the mortgage is on. Consequently, lenders generally prefer that each property mortgaged has its own policy. The exception to this is on portfolio loans, and there are several properties included in one loan.

If you'd like to be a rockstar and your agent's favorite client, please see the new property insurance checklist at the end of this chapter. You can also download it for perpetual reference at www.insuredbyingram.com/download. This contains all of the information that will be needed to get an accurate quote for your new property. Providing this information will probably result in you getting a faster quote because the agent won't need to put in nearly as much time researching public records for the property information.

There are several other types of investment strategies that would also require a dwelling fire policy. These include student housing, assisted living (1-4 units), vacation or short term rentals, and bed and breakfasts. Since the recent rise in bed and breakfasts, several insurance companies have started offering a short-term rental endorsement that may be added to a dwelling fire policy. However, not many standard carriers want to insure these types of investments in the Admitted Market.

For those investors that are interested in these types of investments, I'd like to do a quick, high-level overview of the difference between the Admitted and the Non-Admitted Market. As a rule of thumb, it is best to stay on the Admitted Market. All of the insurance companies that you have likely heard of are considered standard carriers and operate primarily on the admitted market.

The Admitted Market is actively regulated by the state Department of Insurance. As a result, the forms used to create insurance policies are standardized and this market is backed by the state guaranty fund. The state's guaranty fund pays out claims on behalf of the insurance company, should that insurance company become insolvent.

The Non-Admitted Market is regulated by the state Department of Insurance's "surplus lines" and this regulation is far less stringent. Non-admitted insurers are not required to file their forms or rates which affords them much greater flexibility. It allows the Non-Admitted Market to be a great fit for hard-to-place investments and investors that have a heavy claim history. In addition, the Non-Admitted Market is afforded no protection from the state's guaranty fund.

In theory, if the insurance company can not afford to pay out claims, becomes insolvent, or otherwise goes out of business, the state fund will not step in to assist. This is not to say that carriers on the Non-Admitted Market are not financially stable, nor am I saying they are not a viable option. These carriers often play a tremendous role in providing insurance coverage for more difficult investments, such as sober living facilities and other unique and less common investments. Without the Non-Admitted Market, insurance solutions may not be found elsewhere. It is wise, however, to understand the potential risk and less stringent regulations when determining which market is right for you.

If you have any additional questions or want additional information on this chapter, please don't hesitate to reach out to me and I'd be happy to help.

INGRAM INSURANCE

DWELLING FIRE QUOTE

Name: _____

Mailing Address (No PO Boxes): _____

City: _____ State: _____ Zip: _____

Phone Number: _____

E-mail: _____

Number of Properties Owned: _____

Will the property be purchased in an LLC? _____

If so, what is the name of the LLC and how many members? _____

Property Location Address: _____

City: _____ State: _____ Zip: _____

Number of Units (1-4): _____

Year of Construction: _____

Square Feet of building: _____

Purchase Date: _____

Purchase Price: _____

Estimated Rehab Cost (if any): _____

Please e-mail photos of the front and the back of each property to contact@insuredbyingram.com

INSURANCE QUOTE CHECKLIST

What you need to know before talking to your Insurance Agent

- Number of Properties Owned
- Number of Units
- Construction Year
- Estimated years of updates on home (i.e. HVAC, Roof, Electric, Plumbing)
- Building Sq. Feet
- Purchase Date
- Purchase Price
- Estimated Rehab Cost

INGRAM INSURANCE

REHABS, FIX & FLIPS AND THE VACANT POLICY

Vacant policies are more costly than normal dwelling fire and homeowners policies. While a property is vacant, it is much more likely to get broken into, stolen from, or vandalized. Vacant homes also sustain much more damage during fires, as no one is home to call the fire department in a timely matter.

Consequently, the insurance companies want to make sure they are collecting enough premium to offset any claims that may arise due to the heightened risk. When insuring a vacant property, you want to be aware of a few key items and terms. These are minimum earned premium, vandalism and malicious mischief, and calculation of the insurance limits.

Vacant policies commonly come in 3-month, 6-month, or annual terms. Some companies may offer these policies on a monthly basis, but this is less common. When you are insuring property with a vacant policy, you want to be aware of the "minimum earned premium." This is the amount of the premium that will be kept, regardless of how long you have the policy. One of the companies I represent has a 100% minimum earned premium on their 3-month policy. If you insure the policy in this manner, and you have a property for one week and then cancel the policy, you won't get any money back.

Another company has an inspection fee of $100 and that is the only premium that is retained. They also offer a monthly option, so if you were to cancel the policy, you would get all of the unused premiums returned, with the exception of the inspection fee. Depending upon your end-goal, it may make more sense to choose this policy, even if it is more expensive since the minimum earned premium is smaller.

Vandalism and Malicious Mischief is an insurance term commonly abbreviated as "VMM" and is a peril that is commonly excluded on vacant policies. It is also commonly paired with theft. Since vacant properties are not occupied and potentially not checked on regularly, it is easier for rascals to abuse or take advantage of these properties. Some insurance companies do not want to take on this risk and they will exclude this peril, and theft, from the policy.

Most of my clients who utilize these policies are in the midst of a rehab and have someone regularly checking on the property. This isn't as large a deal if someone is regularly at the property. However, it's definitely something in the policy that you want to be aware of. If VMM and theft are excluded, you will want to make sure that you take the appropriate precautions to limit the potential of having these types of losses.

Lastly, figuring out how much to cover the property for is up to the client and their comfort level. Most vacant policies do not offer Replacement Cost coverage. If Replacement Cost is offered, the limit that you will use is most likely going to be what the company's Replacement Cost calculator dictates. However, it is most common for vacant policies to be insured at the Actual Cash Value or the Agreed Value. We have already discussed Actual Cash Value; for this, the limit is generally the purchase price plus the estimated cost of repairs. If a property is purchased for $90,000 and you expect to put $10,000 into the property, we would insure the property for $100,000 using the Actual Cash Value as the settlement option.

Agreed Value is exactly that - a value that both the insured and the insurance company agree the property is worth. Agreed Value is just a means to determine the limit on the amount of coverage on a property. It does not have anything to do with the way a claim or loss would be settled. On an Agreed Value policy, the loss or claim would still be settled at either Actual Cash Value or Replacement Cost.

The last thing to note on vacant policies is that only one property is usually listed on each policy. If your business model only consists of flipping or rehabbing 1-6 properties per year with no more than 2 going on at one time, I would suggest covering your properties using stand-alone policies. If your bandwidth is greater than this, I would start recommending looking into builders risk policies that allow you to blanket the policy over several projects. With these policies, you can either do monthly reporting or add/delete as needed. I'll explain both of these options later for the turnkey folk.

Just like at the end of the dwelling fire chapter, please see the checklist attachment that is slightly different for a vacant policy. This is a quick rundown of all the information that is necessary to provide an accurate quote. If you provide this information on the front end, you'll likely get a quote much faster and also probably become one of your agent's most-loved clients. For future reference, you can download a copy of this at www.insuredbyingram.com/download.

INGRAM INSURANCE

VACANT QUOTE

Name: _____

Mailing Address (No PO Boxes): _____

City: _____ State: _____ Zip: _____

Phone Number: _____

E-mail: _____

Number of Properties Owned: _____

Will the property be purchased in an LLC? _____

If so, what is the name of the LLC and how many members? _____

Property Location Address: _____

City: _____ State: _____ Zip: _____

Number of Units (1-4): _____

Year of Construction: _____

Square Feet of building: _____

Purchase Date: _____

Purchase Price: _____

Estimated Rehab Cost (if any): _____

Scope of work to be completed: _____

_____

Estimated time until complete: _____

Please e-mail photos of the front and the back of each property to contact@insuredbyingram.com

Ingram Insurance Group, LLC. • 118 W First St Suite 312 Dayton, OH 45402 • (937) 310-7205 • contact@insuredbyingram.com

WHOLESALING AND WHOLETAILING

Wholesaling is an art. I'm a huge fan of wholesalers and I have several properties that I have purchased as a result of having a good relationship with them. I couldn't possibly address all caveats or scenarios that wholesalers might run into, so we'll just discuss wholesaling with broad brushstrokes.

As with any business, as soon as you start marketing products or services to anyone, you should already have either a businessowners or general liability policy in force. Most barebones businessowners policies start around $650 per year, and most simple general liability policies are $500 per year. This is a relatively low price to pay for liability protection with limits from $300,000-$1,000,000 per occurrence and $600,000-$2,000,000 annually.

The main difference between a businessowners policy and general liability policy is the included property coverage in the businessowers policy. If you have an office space, you'll most likely want a businessowners policy. This will cover the space, contents, and general liability. If you do not have an office or business property that you wish to insure, a general liability policy will most likely suffice.

The general liability coverage protects the business against liability claims for advertising or personal injury, bodily injury, and property damage. The liability limits on the policy are generally displayed as Per Occurrence and Aggregate. If your policy reads $300,000/$600,000 the policy protects you against the aforementioned claims up to $300,000 Per Occurrence. This limit can include the legal fees, and awarded settlements (in or out of court). If you were to have two incidents in a single year, the Aggregate limit would kick in and grant you a second claim up to $300,000.

For a wholesaler, this coverage could potentially protect against individuals getting hurt while viewing the property or claims the property owner may file against the wholesaler. However, it is highly recommended that you discuss the ins and outs of your business model and investing strategies with your insurance agent to confirm your business is properly covered.

There are many possible scenarios that a wholesaler and wholetailing individual may face. The main issue I'll discuss here is the actual possession of the deed. If you take possession of the deed, you need to get an insurance policy on the particular property as well. If you do not take possession of the deed, the existing owner is responsible for the appropriate insurance.

If you have possession of the deed and the property is not occupied, you'll want to obtain a vacant policy on the property. If you think the property would sell within 3 months, I would highly recommend getting a policy without a small minimum earned premium. Please visit the section on vacant policies to learn more about this type of policy. Similarly, if the property is occupied, you will want to obtain coverage for the property on a dwelling fire policy. Take a look at the section on dwelling fire policies to learn more about them.

APARTMENT COMPLEXES

In the insurance world, any building that has 5 or more residential units is considered a commercial policy. The homeowners, dwelling fires, and vacant policy forms no longer apply to these properties. The insurance terminology for this is commercial habitational or "commercial hab" for short. These properties are generally insured on either a businessowners policy (BOP) or a commercial package policy (CPP). Generally, if the property can be covered on a BOP, the pricing will be the more favorable.

Each insurance company has its own guidelines to follow in order to determine if the property should be written on either a BOP or CPP. These guidelines generally include the age of the buildings, renovation years of the mechanicals (electric, HVAC, plumbing, roof), and exterior finish of the building. These may also include the number of units, the number of stories, and also the presence of smoke detectors or a central fire alarm.

When determining your comfort level for risk on an apartment complex, it is beneficial to be familiar with a few items on your policy. Replacement Cost versus Actual Cash Value, equipment breakdown coverage, loss of income, and ordinance of law.

If you're reading this from start to finish, you're already familiar with the differences between RC versus

ACV, and you can skip the next couple of sections. If you're an apartment investor and flipped through to this chapter, you missed it. You can either flip back to the beginning to find the difference or keep on reading, I've copied and pasted that section below for your convenience.

Settlement Options: Actual Cash Value vs. Replacement Cost

The concept of having insurance revolves around mitigating the risk of loss. If you have a loss, you expect to receive money from the insurance company to return you to the same position you were in prior to that loss - no more, no less. The insurance companies calculate the money that you will receive in a few different ways. The two most common are "Actual Cash Value" and "Replacement Cost." Both of these options are a bit more convoluted than they appear, and neither of them has anything to do with how much you paid for the property. But that's why you're here. So, let's get started.

Replacement Cost

If you call ten different insurance companies, you'll most likely get ten different Replacement Cost Estimates (RCE) for your property. Most insurance companies have Replacement Cost calculators embedded into their websites or quoting systems. These systems gather public information to form an estimate on how much it would cost to rebuild the property - in the event of a total loss - with like materials. The information gathered includes basic residential information such as square feet, number of kitchens, and bathrooms. It also assumes the building materials used given the year of construction. These calculators then factor in the cost of all materials and labor required to rebuild the home exactly as it was originally. This includes outdated materials, inflation, and techniques that may no longer be up to code.

These estimates are also pretty flexible as you can adjust the types of building materials and quality of finish. It generally isn't difficult to increase or decrease these estimates by a few thousand and it generally doesn't affect the premium too greatly.

Here is an example of when this might come into play.

One of the most common drastic changes in older properties is changing the wall type from plaster to drywall. This generally reduces the amount of the Replacement Cost and can have an impact on the amount the policy costs the investor.

To summarize: if you are insuring your property on a Replacement Cost basis, the cost calculation will spit out a number that theoretically represents all the materials and labor needed to get the property back to its original condition.

The replacement cost has nothing to do with the amount that you paid for the property or the amount that you feel the property is worth. For example, I have a duplex that I purchased for $35,000 in 2017. This property is insured at a Replacement Cost of $307,000. If a total loss were to occur - say the building burned to the ground - I would then have a budget of $307,000, which would include demolition, clean-up, materials, and labor necessary to rebuild the property to its condition prior to the fire.

As you're reading this, it's possible that the thought of burning the property down to collect the insurance money crossed your mind. That is exactly why insurance companies are apprehensive about insuring rental properties at replacement cost that were recently acquired for a substantially lower amount than the Replacement Cost calculation.

Insurance companies call this a "moral hazard," and want to do their part in limiting your temptation to commit arson. Depending on the comfort level an insurance company, the condition of the property, or merely the purchase price, you may not be able to get a replacement cost policy until after you have had the property for a few years, or you've made repairs.

Actual Cash Value

The Actual Cash Value formula is an entirely different animal than the replacement cost value. Actual cash value is very commonly abbreviated as ACV, so we are going to do that in this book. Here is the formula: replacement cost - depreciation = actual cash value. A general rule of thumb (not always accurate) to calculate depreciation is 1% per year to a maximum of 50%.

Let's use the example of my duplex again, I purchased it for $35,000 in 2017; it was built in 1900 and the Replacement Cost is $307,000. Since this property was built 119 years ago, it will surpass the max depreciation of 50%. So we will divide 307,000 by 2 to get $153,500.

In the event of a total loss, like the building burning down, I would receive a check for $153,500. Most likely, this would not replace the structure as it stands, and it would not be sufficient to rebuild. However, I could use this to clean up the mess, sell the land, and purchase another similar property.

As we are speaking in terms of a total loss, the difference between ACV and RC is just a matter of how much money you'll be walking away with. In my opinion, the largest exposure and difference between the different settlement options comes in the event of a partial loss. Let us continue building on the previous example, but change it to a partial loss instead of a total loss.

A kitchen-fire destroys the kitchen in one of the two units. In order to complete all of the repairs, it would cost $45,000. This is within both the RC limit of $307,000 and ACV limit of $153,500. Under the Replacement Cost policy, you would receive the entire amount of $45,000 and you would probably end up with a much nicer kitchen than you started off with.

However, with the ACV policy, depreciation will be factored into the loss. If we were to apply the rule of thumb, the total amount would be adjusted with a 50%

decrease. Under the ACV policy, you would receive around $27,500 to make the repairs.

Some investors that have either dedicated contractors or who do the work themselves are comfortable with this. There isn't a right or wrong way to pick your policy. It all depends on how much risk you are willing to shoulder and take responsibility for.

As an insurance agent, it is always easier to recommend clients to go with the Replacement Cost policy. You'll get better coverage and in the event of a loss, you will most likely receive more money than it takes to repair the property. If you have an ACV policy and you're not fully aware of the implications, you may potentially be very upset at the time of a loss.

Just remember that, depending on the price and condition of the property, an ACV policy may be your only option until you've either seasoned the property or made the appropriate repairs.

Equipment Breakdown coverage is included in many businessowners policies and commercial package policies. This coverage is for any equipment attached to the apartment complex. This can include HVAC, boilers, or computers and copiers - if you have a front office in the apartment complex. Equipment breakdown covers mechanical and electrical breakdown of these items and the coverage is applied to the repair or the replacement of the equipment.

In apartment complexes, the mechanicals can be very expensive. These items are generally accounted for in the percentage you set aside for capital expenditures. Prior to submitting any claim for equipment breakdown, it would be advantageous to check with your provider to see if the claim will count against you.

Some insurance companies offer equipment breakdown coverage and the claims filed for this coverage will never be factored into the premiums that you pay. If this is the case, it may be beneficial to utilize this coverage. However, if the claim will count as any other claim, I would not recommend using this coverage. Filing too many claims could either cause your coverage to be nonrenewed or adversely affect your premium. From a long-term perspective, utilizing your CapEx reserves would be most advantageous.

Ordinance or law coverage is often unexplained and often not added to policies. The definition of ordinance or law coverage, from the International Risk Management Institute, www.IRMI.com is as follows:

"Coverage for loss caused by enforcement of ordinances or laws regulating construction and repair of damaged buildings. Older structures that are damaged may need upgraded electrical; heating, ventilating, and air-conditioning (HVAC); and plumbing units based on city codes. Many communities have a building ordinance(s) requiring that a building that has been damaged to a specified extent (typically 50 percent) must be demolished and rebuilt in accordance with current building codes rather than simply repaired. Unendorsed, standard commercial property insurance forms do not cover the loss of the undamaged portion of the building, the cost of demolishing that undamaged portion of the building, or the increased cost of rebuilding the entire structure in accordance with current building codes. However, coverage for these loss exposures is widely available by endorsement. Standard homeowners policies include a provision granting a limited amount of building ordinance coverage; this amount can be increased by endorsement. Also referred to as building ordinance coverage."

The ordinance or law coverage is most beneficial for older apartment complexes. The example I often use here in Ohio is electrical outlets. Ohio has many apartments and homes that still have ungrounded two-prong outlets. If a partial loss occurred and ordinance or law coverage was not purchased, the policy would only cover replacing the building in its present condition.

Any extra-incurred expenses in grounding the outlets would likely not be covered. This coverage is sometimes included in policies and must be requested on others; please do your due diligence in determining your need and coverage.

Now let's go over common coverages and sections on individual policies. These include building limits, liability limits for each occurrence and aggregate, limits for damage to premises rented to you, fire legal liability, medical expense, personal and advertising injury, and products completed.

Building limits are the prescribed amount that the insurance will not exceed. Lenders often want to be sure this amount is at least equivalent to the amount of the loan. As an investor, you'll want to make sure that this amount will at least pay back any loan, clean up the debris, and also repay you any money that you have invested. Please be sure you understand Actual Cash Value and Replacement Cost.

Liability limits for Per Occurrence and Aggregate values limit how much the insurance company will pay out per incident per year. Aggregate is generally calculated on an annual term; the Aggregate limit is often twice the per-incident limit. Consequently, you'd likely be covered for two incidents within the same annual policy period. However, we should genuinely hope you never have to use the Aggregate limit.

Damage to premises rented to you covers damage to property or areas that are rented to you. The International Risk Management Institute (www.irmi.com) states, "It applies to damage by fire to premises rented to the insured and to damage regardless of cause to premises (including contents) occupied by the insured for 7 days or less. The basic limit is $100,000." This limit is usually much lower than the others; in apartment investing, you are not likely to come across this coverage.

Fire legal liability is a coverage that I often get questions about. This coverage is generally not applicable to apartment owners. When the named insured is a tenant at a location, this coverage would cover the fire damage to the rented property caused by the tenant - the named insured. More often than not, you can completely ignore this coverage on your policy as the chances of you having a claim that invokes this coverage is slim. The follow-up question I get is if removing it will lower the premium. Unfortunately, the answer is no - this coverage cannot be removed from the policy form.

Medical expense coverage is the same here as it is on your home, auto, or dwelling fire policy. This coverage pays for any immediate medical expenses of individuals that get injured on your property. This coverage is often used immediately to attempt to prevent larger liability claims in the future. This commonly comes in $5,000 increments. Please make sure you have enough medical expense coverage to feel comfortable that it is sufficient to cover immediate medical expenses.

Personal and advertising injury was previously two separate coverages - personal injury and advertising injury - but they've been combined since 1986. I'll once again allow the International Risk Management Institute (www.IRMI.com) to define these coverages. IRMI states that advertising injury is, "A general liability coverage, combined in standard commercial general liability (CGL) policies with personal injury (PI) coverage, that insures the following offenses in connection with the insured's advertising of its goods or services: libel, slander, invasion of privacy, copyright infringement, and misappropriation of advertising ideas." Personal injury includes, "false arrest, detention, or imprisonment; malicious prosecution; wrongful eviction; slander; libel; and invasion of privacy. Also addressed in the homeowners policy. Under umbrella liability insurance, a broad category of insurable offenses that includes both BI and the offenses defined as "personal injury" in CGL policies."

Up last is products-completed coverage. This is important coverage for apartment owners to be familiar with because it is largely used for contractors. It covers liability claims that may arise after the products and work completed by a contractor are finished. An example of this would be if a mold remediation company were hired to eradicate mold and it came back later and caused sickness. This is one of the many reasons that you should obtain proof of insurance for all contractors that do work for your business.

TURNKEY PROVIDERS

Providing turnkey properties to real estate investors is an awesome business model. Especially for out-of-state investors that wish to take advantage of different real estate markets. Most investors that do rehabs, fix-and-flips, or even buy-and-hold can be taken care of just fine on vacant and dwelling fire policies.

If a turnkey provider has a dedicated staff member and hard-working insurance agent, turnkey providers can also utilize the same policies. However, it may be a better and less intense option for the turnkey provider to get a builders risk policy that allows for several properties to be scheduled on one policy. This is commonly referred to as a blanket policy, and commonly incorrectly called an "umbrella" policy.

The blanket builders risk policies generally come in two different options: monthly reporting and add/delete. If you are a turnkey provider that really cranks out properties and has several open projects at once, it is probably in your best interest to choose the monthly reporting option. Otherwise, the add/delete option will most likely be sufficient.

Under the monthly reporting option, once each month, you will send in a report that includes properties owned, newly acquired properties, open projects and estimated total cost, recently finished projects, and properties sold. All of these changes will be recorded and the premiums will be adjusted accordingly. Failure to submit a report on a monthly basis can negatively impact coverages due to information on locations being inaccurate and or out of date.

These policies include a coverage and limit for properties recently acquired between monthly reporting. Once you reach a certain threshold of production, this manner of reporting becomes easier than handling several stand-alone policies. You'll know when your company is ready to make the switch.

The add/delete option follows the same concept but doesn't have the same monthly reporting structure. When you acquire a policy, you'll notify the insurance agent to add the property to the policy. When you finish a project, you'll have it deleted from the builders risk if sold, or transferred to a dwelling fire policy if kept as a rental.

In addition to the builders risk policies for the projects, it would be wise to also have either a businessowners policy (BOP) or a general liability (GL) policy. This was briefly covered in the chapter for wholesalers and wholetailers. As a quick recap, if you market products or services to anyone, it is wise to have a BOP or GL policy. If you have an office space with contents that you'd like covered, a BOP would better suit you. If you do not have any office space or contents that you'd like covered, a GL policy will most likely meet your needs.

THE IMPORTANCE OF RENTERS INSURANCE

At this point, we've covered the basics of insurance you need for your investment strategy. However, if you have any residential property, it is imperative that you require all of your residents to carry renters insurance. If you do not, you are leaving yourself and your business incredibly exposed.

Renters insurance is often marketed to the actual residents, your tenants. Because of this, common knowledge is that the policy is for providing insurance on the residents' belongings in the event of a covered loss. Consequently, when I have this conversation with investors, they're quick to tell me how little they care for the tenant's contents and belongings. You may relate to this sentiment...but, not so fast!

Renters policies are written on the same form as a homeowners policy. The main difference is that the actual building and structure is not covered on the policy. The liability portion of the policy is what investors need to be interested in.

As we've discussed, the liability portion of the renters policy covers liability claims (per event and per year) and there are coverage limits for medical expenses.

This creates a giant liability buffer between the residents, their guests, and your insurance policy.

For example, let's say your resident has a guest over and the classic trip and fall occurs. If your resident has an active renters policy, the first liability claim will hit the renters insurance policy. At this point, in order for the claim to make it to your policy, they'd have to prove the cause of the trip was the investor's negligence, not the residents lack of maintenance or upkeep (which they're contractually responsible for according to your lease).

Similarly, the renters policy will be the first line of defense for property damage. If the resident is cooking a delicious meal and accidentally sets the kitchen on fire and causes damage, this will first be covered by their renters policy. Now, if the resident is intentional on setting fire to your property, that is a completely different story and it is not likely to be covered under their policy.

Verifying that your resident has a valid insurance policy falls solely in your hands. What you do to confirm that your residents have their own insurance policy must be consistent and enforceable. If a claim occurs and no renters policy is in force, it is too late.

The chances of the insurance company attempting to pursue the resident as an individual is very slim. From my experience, even though your lease contractually requires the resident to carry a renters policy, your insurance company will not enforce it.[11] The lease and requirement to carry a renters policy is yours and yours alone to enforce. Most insurance companies get nervous and want to cancel or non-renew your policy if you have 2 claims in a single year. I have clients that have upwards of 2,000 units. Statistically, this magnifies the importance of having checks and balances for renters insurance in place.

Unfortunately, there isn't currently an easy way to go about doing this. You can request to be listed as either an additional insured or additional interest on their policy; however, you are then relying on the insurance company to notify you via snail mail when the policy cancels. This requires that it not be lost either en route or in your pile of other mail. You can also request a declaration page that shows the policy is active and current; however, after you see it, they can cancel it or stop paying it.

I'm in the process of working with a few insurance companies to create a master policy that an investor has positive control over and can list all of his or her properties and residents onto the policy. While this would require adding the cost to the resident's rent, the investor would be responsible for making the monthly premium payment. However, you'd have 100% confidence that all of your residents have renters insurance and that most liability events that happen to your property are buffered by your tenants.

---

[11] However, if your lease requires renters insurance and they don't, if a kitchen fire or something else occurs, you can sue the renter to recoup some of your expenses. It may end up being your only recourse.

If you're interested in this, please email me and let me know at ryan@insuredbyingram.com. I'll keep you up to date on the progress and when the product will be available.

BRINGING IT ALL TOGETHER

Thanks for taking the time to read this book, I hope you've learned a great deal and are now confident to go out and have an educated conversation as you are selecting your insurance policies. As I've said from the beginning, I'm hooked on this stuff. I'll never turn down a conversation about real estate investing and I'm absolutely thrilled that I can provide a service and protection for other investors and their portfolios.

I find a great deal of joy in taking rundown properties with tons of deferred maintenance, bringing new life into them, and providing a family with an awesome place to live. I pay a higher price and receive a lower return in order to keep my properties free from deferred maintenance so the residents may have at least some pride in rentership.

I'm a huge advocate of always doing the right thing simply because it is the right thing to do. I feel so strongly on this that I have passed up several opportunities to include deals and large clients that would have meant a great deal (monetarily) to my family. I'd much rather keep my character and integrity intact than prosper from doing a disservice to anyone. There is simply too much to go around for everyone to think otherwise.

Similarly, I focus on the relationships with my Lord Jesus Christ, my wife, children, and friends. I'm working as hard as I can on a daily basis to build a legacy for my children and children's children; but, I will not sacrifice the present moment I have with my loved ones for a future payoff with the potential of them not being around.

I mention all of this, not to pat myself on the back, but to allow you to see into my thoughts and decision-making process. In a nutshell, this is my heart. If you feel similarly, and want to work hard to establish a solid base of residual income to create a legacy and protect it for centuries to come, I'm with you. I want to be on your team, help you grow, and share all of my resources and knowledge with you. Since you've read this book, I imagine this strikes a chord with you. You're most likely on the path to learn all that you can to better your future.

One of my clients shares these thoughts and we have spent a lot of time talking about similar things. On one of the properties he recently acquired, the insurance came back and stated they were going to exclude the roof unless it was replaced. He understood and admitted it was an older roof with a bunch of patchwork, though it wasn't leaking. He made a call and had it replaced within two weeks. He understood that this would be a long-term investment and he plans on keeping this as an income-producing property for decades. Consequently, he is going to have to replace the roof again at some point.

While I don't expect this of everyone, if this doesn't resonate with you and you'd prefer to increase your margins by deferring maintenance, we most likely will not be a good fit. Unfortunately, I'm familiar with "investors" that allow residents to live in homes with holes in the roof, flooded basements, vegetation overtaking the home. The list goes on and on. These folks have told me that they bought the home for $16,000 it is in a D neighborhood and will never be worth more. Consequently, they'll rent it out for $400 per month until the market dictates otherwise. Then they'll drop the rent put another person in that is "one step above homeless." If this repulses you, we will get along just fine.

I've said this several times before, but it couldn't be more true, I can't wait to speak to you and hear about your real estate investing goals and dreams. I'm looking forward to doing my part in helping you build and protect your legacy for generations to come. Since you've read this book, I imagine this strikes a chord with you.

I'm looking forward to helping and speaking with you. If there is any doubt in your mind on whether or not you should reach out to me, choose yes. It'll be the highlight of my workday to talk with you about real estate: Ryan@insuredbyingram.com.

In the meantime, keep learning, bettering yourself, and creating the best of all possible lives for your family and the best of all possible communities for your city.

ACKNOWLEDGEMENTS

This book and knowledge was developed and gleaned via countless hours of those much smarter and more helpful than I. I'd like to give a special thanks to Jim Grushon and Gwen Price. Thank you both for introducing me to and teaching me a great deal about property and casualty insurance. More importantly, thank you for all that you have done for and provided to my family over the years. You two are truly loved.

In the local Dayton area, I'd like to thank Peter Julian, Darrin Carey, and Paul Amegatcher. You three have added incalculable value to my life and family. Thanks for all the lessons and guidance. I wouldn't be halfway where I am without all of the time you all have taken away from your day to teach me the ways of investing and calling me out when I make silly decisions.

Lindsey Carpenter and Kourtney Yoder, thanks for being the most awesome marketing reps out there. You've raised the bar and set the standards for all the other carriers!

Seth Buechley and Rich Allen, thanks for continually working with me and helping me refine who I am as a Christian, husband, father, and businessmen. My family is better off because I have had the honor of knowing you.

Darrin Schenck, thanks for being my coach for over a decade now. Thanks for always pushing me, holding me accountable, and never letting me make excuses.

Wil, thanks for being the best brother I could ask for. Thanks for never letting me settle and always giving me the courage to be the best person I can be. With you in my corner, I haven't got a fear.

ABOUT THE AUTHOR

Ryan Ingram is a Christ follower, husband (to a wife way out of his league), father of 2 kids (and counting!), real estate investor, insurance agent, and overall serial entrepreneur. He has started and sold several companies before falling helplessly in love with real estate. As a hobby, he loves having conversations about real estate investing. Professionally, he loves helping others grow their portfolios and educate them on how to protect their portfolios to secure financial freedom.

Ryan loves hearing from other investors, to stay in touch with him subscribe to his e-mail list at insuredbyingram.com. Alternatively, tune in to the Insurance for Real Estate Investors Podcast or e-mail him directly at ryan@insuredbyingram.com

JOIN THE CONVERSATION!

Before you let this book collect dust on your bookshelf, don't forget to take advantage of the free downloads at www.insuredbyingram.com/download. These downloads include insurance checklists, an infographic that helps walk you through which type of insurance policy you need, and visual explanations of different insurance terms and coverages.

Though I think this book reveals the basics about insurance for real estate investors, this is an ever changing industry. Sign up for the email list to stay up to date on articles I regularly publish specifically for investors.

Lastly, please remember I completely love talking about all things related to real estate investing. If you have any questions that you'd like for me to answer, or just want to talk about different markets and investing strategies, shoot me an email! I'd love to help and looking forward to meeting you!

www.ingramcontent.com/pod-product-compliance
Lightning Source LLC
Chambersburg PA
CBHW030533210326
41597CB00014B/1135